The Blackbird

Pamela Coren was born in Rochdale in 1949. She holds degrees in literature from East Anglia, London and Leicester Universities and has published academic work on Spenser, Campion, Donne and Jonson. Pamela Coren is currently researching the modernist poets' rediscovery of early music. Her poetry has appeared in a number of poetry magazines and she was recognised in the 2001 National Poetry Competition. She is married to David Coren and lives in Stamford, in Lincolnshire.

THE BLACKBIRD INSPECTOR

Pamela Coren

Laurel Books

First published in 2005 by
Laurel Books
282 The Common Holt Wiltshire BA14 6QJ

Printed by
Antony Rowe Ltd
Bumpers Farm Chippenham Wiltshire SN14 6QA

© Pamela Coren, 2005

The rights of Pamela Coren as author of this work
are asserted in accordance with Section 77 of the
Copyright, Designs and Patents Act 1988

A CIP record for this book is available from the
British Library

ISBN 1-873390-07-6

To David

Grateful acknowledgement is due to the editors of the following magazines where some of these poems first appeared:

Agenda, Aireings, Dreamcatcher, The Interpreter's House, Iota, Magma, Poetry Nottingham International, Raindog, The Reader, Reactions 4, Rialto, Smiths Knoll.

POEMS

THE BLACKBIRD INSPECTOR

THE BLACKBIRD INSPECTOR

I've been on the case since dawn. Even now
my men are sifting the woods, bagging up
small bones like flutes. Some report messages
in Gaelic; others find evidence in caves
and clefts in the rock. There are claims
that larger primates turn their ears to them,
and children open their eyes from the cot.

Listen again to the original, amplified
and slowed — now: do you hear that?
The syntax is of no taught mythology:
it has darkness in it, and slow beats,
and intervals shaved finer than ours.

From the oak and holly, in the wet leaves
she utters it calmly, again and again,
across distance, close; a voiced tambourine
trembling the balance of the inner ear.

I've had to suspend all routine operations,
be-rhymed by it, chanted down
by the common secret messenger,
given over to the history of woods
where so much is buried, where her gullet
disgorges layered codes of stolen land,
flung momentary lives, instances of slippage
from unmarked files gone to rags in leafmould.

No public benefit, admitted, in saxon crime,
but under the clearing to find that final note,
the unsolved sudden rise — I'll nail that yet.

THE HOPPING SONG

I saw her once
Hop forty paces through the public street

Enobarbus

Oh no you should not, lady
not that lopsided leaping
that furious strenuous kangarooing
down the hallooing street falling
and not falling over and over
tiara slopped over one eye
for the elegance of thigh
is for the senators a stillness
a repose of observation — it
oh no — it don't have places to go
with this joke of a crotch stretched
all the world looking, sideways peeping

for we want you in the camera
in the frame in the stills standing
not hop hop hopping
like a mad jack rabbit
smelling the green juice of spring
down in the marsh all of a hop
with toads and locusts
swarming every Nile mile —

and if you carry on so
we'll all be caught on the
        hop   all skivers, all no-hopers
all on the hop from senator-school

but we'll follow, lean lolloping lady,
like a kid on the flags with a slippy stone,
no ceiling above, no brick walls round,
chalking up schemes on the scruffy ground
with a toe-spring, a knee-fling; make it home,
one foot square on the nose of Caesar.

THE FLOWER-MAIDEN OF THE MABINOGIAN

Flowers of oak, broom and meadowsweet,
minute, yellow and pale yellow,
compact and cream to a flesh.

To touch her is to be swept senseless
by the living earth. Under the petal skin
brown fibres and husks, sepals and leafage,
fresh and dying blossoms trail and wind
to a tender mass, humus rich.

She feels the soreness of roots trailing,
weakness of a stalk holding itself upright,
cells craving the surge of water. Eyes and ears
were poorly magicked. She scarcely sees,
bathed in a maze of tissued light.

Her pores feel each tiny pressure of air.
The fibrous brain holds her together,
driving and pulsing, opens a pineal
to the light. She keeps steady on footsoles
soft, flax-woven, sensing the ribs of grass.

Inside she flexes whips, red-orange heat
flickering up the stems: from her face
yellow rays shoot the horizon,
blinding magicians, husbands
eager to offer their hopeless baptism.

VENUS AT WICKEN FEN

Wicken drinks
silky woven light
laced with little trout,
set with minnow silver.
Still as the sun
and the high slips of cloud
the water waits and sips,
puts cool lips up to damselflies.

On either side the wooden bridge
a lime and lemon waterworld;
frog-green plates, white & yellow cups
teeter on slim stems. Fans of leaf
touch fingers, wave secret messages.

Looking in we shrink and swim the mind
in centimetre rooms of sway and green.
We would put out our arms
to let this liquid lift us, tiny as fish,
and with one flick of feet slide
quiet into watercaves,
float under green fibre crossings
lucid as the sky.

The girls come from the boat
in bathing suits with rubber rings:
one bombs off the bridge
and sends a wave of fat and power
through every interlock of leaf and water;
the mudbed shudders her frank arrival;
the pool scales up her shrieks
to Veronese's opera madonnas.

She belts the water boisterous,
breasts and arms MacDonalds slick,
wallows delighted in her icy licking heaven,
while altogether bonier and dry we watch
the rapt Queen rise.

Flesh buys up the waterworld: flushes
rosy up Monk's Lode, through reedy waters,
bores past the birding men with bulging glasses
who wonder for an ignorant moment
what goose, what duck of alien illustration
sings such high song in Wicken's brackish wet.

ONIONS TO ANGELS

Devilish slippery gift
wrapped tight in pink crackle.
Cheap, reliable, shaped to your hand.
Kitchen globular Muse,
Falstaff on the tongue,
unfettered sweet-to-the-core
soft & sweating godlessness.

Runs you to earth,
warm as a chicken in a dust bowl,
races the acrid blood
under your delicate and proper skin,
leads you laughing
through luminous layers of vesty flesh
leaving no chink for ghosts.

In the thin pip of the heart
signs off the vaguely entailed inheritance,
wafts away the chemical committee
of adjusted odour, the stink of perfection.

Under your knife a rude-rich presence
riots, sends all the watery angels weeping off.

NOT GOING TO MORRISONS

I took the Micra to its MOT,
where cars are lined up neatly on the gravel —
the town behind us with its stone-bright alleys,
the garage lady walking with her clipboard
pleasant and polite: *Will you stay? About an hour . . .*

declined the proffered plastic waiting room
and walked across the way to Morrisons,
but turned aside to where a dusty track
leads to the flex of our flat-country river,
the brown and easy Welland flirting by.

Cows stood in the river: thick and furry knees
launched little floats of cud and stumbled mud.
I sat by ash and willow, sloe and elder,
with thorn and thistle, teasle, reed and rush.
The river sloped along and asked for nothing back.

A cricket leapt and threaded through the grass,
and next a small bug like a leaf on springs,
a buzzing fly, a dragonfly in blue and gold,
a late and heavy bee. The river shelves
were packed to overflowing, slipped and tangled.

Along the wood-edge path the rabbits dropped
in hollows made of dust. Swallows shot up
to queue along the wire, and then began to sing,
rifling the cowpat meadows and each corner of the sky
above the practice of the Uffington estate.

Slow afternoon gave out its balm of rose-bay
and space between the clouds and grass lay
like a cool castle's long-abandoned armoury.
I went back for the car, which passed, and, driving,
saw, bursting above Morrisons, rooks at two-for-one.

DELIVERY OF THE DAMP PATCH

In the corner where only the Hoover goes,
where the Yucca dries and crinkles,
a chemical arrival, a soft iota. Gratis.

Just one in our new unnumbered series,
sent direct upon your least expression.
It's easy to unfold: one grain whispers
its silent cipher in a file of shades,
green of the primeval beach,
grey dust of fallen keeps.

Later, the sweep of its contours
will study your desire, taste the sigh
roaming your boundaries; from there
our delicate tints will lead you
from the laminate grey insurance suite

to the land of gills, where breath laces
green tendrils with silver beads, threads
shilly-shallying up to the press of air
to detonate cartoon ideas, to burble
wanton speech of heroes, pointing you
to where you could have gone and didn't,
when water was your skin, your go-between
before the stark geography of flesh
dried you out flat like starfish on a shelf.

Should your property values diminish
upon receipt of our product, rest assured
you were born not to office but to joy,
and nothing stands secure
against our small print's slow translation
of you, as yet unfathomed, here to there.

MONDAY'S ST. GEORGE

Up the stone steps comes the hot breath,
the sound of great feet possing, possing,
wet slap of hide on the floor,
creak and groan of the hinged wings.

When we go down it froths and hides,
too slippery to handle. Instead
we play with Mum's fighting gear,
the copper and the fearful gas jet,
the wooden grabbing tongues.

She works on its writhing with warm hands,
mottled red: comes up from the fray
with damp pinny and hair in a frizz.

It wrestles till dark, flapping free of skin,
scales, damp and harsh; steams away
in time for Dad's home-from-work tea.

Tuesday, the cellar's a lair of cooling zinc,
condensed sunlight. The slabbed floor's
claw scraped, smells of stone from the moor.

MY FATHER IN THE HILLS

A strata line in a lump of slate recalls him,
precise, thin, wandering into crumb, shale,
a bronze thread in the stone, bitten off.

And the distant hill which may be a cloud
or it may be the one we're trying for
on the brown map gone thick with finding.

I remember the grief of a child, shock
that slithered and unwound its coils
into red eyes and saw broken things.

The dreams of coffins were unreal:
coffins do not fall out of pantries
or rear up sudden from cellar slabs.

I do not know if it was his, or hers,
or where the child went: in the end
I slept. Having no hands but scales

I can't grasp much of a father, but
in the mirror familiar lines crumble,
child, woman, man, the same eyes

tensed on distant detail, things that are
exact and disappear like deer-tracks,
the mortise turn, exit, the no more of things.

BONFIRE AT EIGHT

What do you eat, my crackling pony
swinging your head in the garden?
Stick and weed and paper bag,
box and leaf and canvas shred.

What do you eat, my sparking prince,
crowning the air in the garden?
Your past, your waste, your boring days,
your hours of sloth and sadness.

THE END OF ORPHEUS

At first light he dreams of silver strings
stretched from heart to horizon, reaches
through river-mist to pluck a chord.

At his finger ends the first bird raves.
His music sets off sunrise, looses
hoarded colours into the floodplain.

He plays each damp thing into light,
articulates the willows and the sedge,
trims the feather lines on the lapwing.

But wakes to himself in the river,
hair fanned in the current, a seeing eye
caught and eddying in the breeze.

Dream plays back the cells of his body,
lengthens the nerves of his wanderings,
man-god heroics and the charm of Sirens,

dismembered love located note by note,
from the tricky places of dedication
to the last dropping of the hand.

Now his name is locked inside a head
singing words for unsounded waters,
building a church of memory, mere notes

of a brain conceiving, as if his long desire
for strings and their voluptuous finger-kiss
could ever lull itself to words. He cries on death,

but what the woman-frenzy left persists,
cerebral godhead drifting down Hebrus,
mysteries washing from his neck, entrancing

islands, long trade routes, sailors setting out
to net the spices reeking from his mouth, trace
the silver wash of high harmonics in the blood.

MID-LENT FAIR

Grudging elders nevertheless observe
the ritual of spring. Keep out the cars,
bring in the cars. A Wild West gambling shack
jams up against the Collyweston sag,
Vortex and Ultimate Experience plunge
a calculated inch past medieval mullions.

Broad Street packs the house of colour in,
springs it open. Out on the seamed palm
jump our kids, candy jangling in the mud.
They've saved all year for this. Not sulking now,
they leap above the spires, howling down the rain,
testing the heart's stopping distance, the night fuse.

History whoops in the alleys: good to see
Old Fool's still here, and the shining Juggler.

THE OLD GAME

Scary, that weapon winding on its tall spring,
shell and spine of a tower, mill with no sails,
staircase with no steps, wicker man, totem,
blank lighthouse looming high over the pier.
Can it hold back the sea — seige machine
hoiked to the very edge of winter waves?

Gnomes lurk, cajoling and grimacing
on the hidden stair. It is a dark climb:
it is us they trap, one by one in our curiosity.

Pell mell into the cell bundle him, trundle him
and out of the window harum scarum him
helter skelter, fear no colours, course him, trounce him

but you land with your mat like a cat,
all your lives ringing and singing inside you.

JACK'S PROGRESS

Jack snugs,
deep in his folds,
muffles his piercing bellows-cry.

Jack tenses
for his moment of fame,
scrolled
in his inheritance,
safe in approval
of his terrifying ways.

He's like his cousin Punch
in nose and chin and roaring cheeks,
and oh, the dreadful cap,
the cock, the comb
springing like a vicious tongue.

If Jack emerges
(and there is wear on the rivets)
see him, one seven league boot
bounding across Suffolk fields,
rain softening his colours,
rusting his coils. Jack,
gazing by still waters.

Is he happy, an alright Jack,
or will he creak slowly, sadly back,
flit through the ginnels,
crouch by the dustbins,
and in through the window
in one fell spring,
hapless hands flapping at the catch?

ANYONE WOULD HAVE THOUGHT IT
A QUIET FUNERAL

The hearse lifts its tailgate to the porch
to bring in this father who lived largely in affections,
who came to meeting when he wanted to,
and now we gather softly to support the family
of a man we've tried all week to recollect,
arriving at a back-row presence
we somehow knew to be kind, but with no
strident list of certainties to bolster him to
in the usual constructing of the dead

and with few words said, no more
than would comfort grandchildren,
we're pleased that no prepared eulogy
molests the man whose face we just recall
while we toy with what we do
and don't believe, trying to be good

and not admit to our meeting selves
that we would like a ride in this gentle cot,
grey rubber wheels bumping the threshold,
the burden of white flowers on our breast,
and nose-deep in fresh lilies and roses
lie back in the space under the window,
leaves rustling on the glass,
sunlight pouring down like a great horn,

and never again form well-meaning words,
but let the face drop its tiresome practice
to put on the peace
of a man who held his palms out
to love entirely
what he was given to love.

A BAG OF USEFUL THINGS

2lb of patchwork pieces, coloured threads,
and strong needles, 100. 9 darning.
A Bible, in plain binding. An ounce of pins.
Everything the best we can manage, Friend,
for I hear the climate can be extreme.
9 balls of sewing cotton. Scissors, bodkin,
staylaces, thimble, good soap, pair of spectacles.
We do not know what is provided there.
We do not know enough. Only that the line
goes on, bruised and dirty, babies at suck.
We cannot stop it. We can bag up a desperate
small beginning. I do not know if the hope
transports with them, or stays with us.

"A bag of useful things" — one of the forms of Quaker relief
work among women prisoners sentenced to transportation

A BAG OF USELESS THINGS

I kept a close grip on the other bag —
not the regular sewing kit, Bible, handkerchief one
pressed into my hand at the dock,
but the one with the skeleton leaf,
the cracked mirror, the sparrow skull,
the clutch of hawthorn berries,
the paper of snuff,
the driftwood knot;
the little bag
that rustled at my side, richest silk
torn from the skirts of one they hanged,
drawn tight with a twist of adder's hide,
weighted with pennies, two for my eyes.

COMPLAINT OF THE AGEING ANATOMY

Melancholy man broods, wrist to jaw —

Complex, crisp, articulate,
I offer vision clean from the socket,
deep silence, stillness of the ribs.
In the rock of the spine I hold final truth,
unembarrassed, faultless.

She's chosen else: tissue, rolls, threads,
grotesque particulars, lines running back
beyond our marriage. She stares in mirrors,
taps her cheeks, trying to catch me out.

I could retort — who supported her so long? —
but she sees the cage of me and I'm lost.
I have no trick of tendering, only
I could show her the dawn,
my own inheritance of pearly light.
I could glow in the dark and tell tales
beside the fireside, but she won't hear,
so little of me in those worms of sound
spiralling in. She thins like sinking water.
Curled up on cushions, asks for laughter.

Does no-one hear me,
jaw cracking like pistol shots?

IN THE ARMS OF MORPHEUS

who's the guy with a million fingers,
who can lay light pearls on each pore,
rest his long limbs along yours so gentle
he's in your mouth and down between your toes
and just a breath away.

This guy has a sighing way in your ears
can loosen the night hours, murmur
the flakes of dark into star scales.

He's got foreplay from the luxury pack,
licks the small muscles to soften
the corners of your lips, eases
the salt of watching from your eyes.

Like the swan rocks the river
the beat of his glide is in your breastbone
until the deep hours.

And when it comes to the real show
and he slides into his harbour
he's the only guy you'll ever find
with world enough,
and space, and time.

TWO FANTASIAS ON THE BODY AS JOKESTER

1 GLASS SKELETON

Rakish resident, clicks heels in the dawn,
conjures on ice-brink, aqua tinted rods
worn to a shine; angles, stalks free in air,
flares sad in cupboards, betrayed by dark.

Fragile, needs to dance, fears sitting out,
suffering afflatus of tubes and fibres. Restless
in the committees of men. Do not bring it
to the hammer, the smash of reflection.

It will jig into place to its own glockenspiel,
articulate apparition, clown of night:
cold as the sea when the berg slips its root.
Alone it sings of heaven, sees magical things.

Melt kills: under the ribs the prick of truth,
unique crystal, rig of light, time's freeze.

2 BLOOD RIVER

Close-packed, unnatural landscape: given,
for our subsistence, a pump in a well,
a mesh of irrigation. Channels seep
and sigh at fibrous ends and subtle knots.

Currents deepen and trench to muddy courses:
make confluence at silted junctions. Lately
the river runs to estuary in the hands,
a little blue, a little ropy after much travel.

In the heat of desultory beds the river practises,
lowers sluices, dreams a tempest. Its knock
wakes us, anxious at three am, but it's friendly,

fitted with engines for temperance, each Pinchbeck
and Pode Hole measuring the outfall to Lethe,
murmuring a liquid self, fluent in the dark.

COMING HOME FROM THE PUB TO BAD NEWS

We must have passed the beginning
on the way somewhere else, as entrylocks
need memory to run against the clock
and the late beer in the bar
where lads built for rugby
shout each other down. From the wall
the other country beasts curl their horns
and glass their eyes, helpless.
In the dislocation of the match
we pick things up awkwardly,
trying to pitch it right, never quite hearing,
but smile into our pints. It'll be fine,
just this offside mud pressured up the veins
and into stark daylight in glass measures,
hours dripping into the tray by the bed
where he fights the clock to get in, or out,
hurling his ghost against the beastly scrum
for his frail possession, his name on the chart,
the purse in his pocket and the small change
scrabbled up
from this malty brew, this light-headed dark.

NOT SUFFERING THE MIDNIGHT OWL

Don't come near me, Mr. Owl,
with your hooter, your clock,
your creepy talents.
I don't want to know
about crop failure, plague, war,
about the loss of lawsuits.
Stuff your motorway crashes,
your lost children, your footsie index.

Your pinion feathers caress me
solicitously. I don't want to feel
the brown feathers and the white
tickling my ear. I can feel
my nose twitch in terror,
my legs shrink to the long splay feet
of the undergrowth, the leaf cover.

Turn your mad head away,
right round to the day you came from
when you stole the sun and ate it.
I see it bulge in your head,
swelling your eyes round the yellow point,
the arrow-slit where the barons shot my father
for running, man, for running.

MY LOVE IS LIKE A CHRISTMAS TREE

Your various decorations worn vociferous
at myriad tips offer to wave, twirl and tremble
defter than any tree of standard blossom.
Bric a brac of arts and nations, not abandoning
mother's plastic star or the paper twists of children
roost with gestures of ancient craft, with poised
delicacies of tinsel origami in the coolest style,
and your speciality is that each lights the other,
light being your bristling kingdom. Candle ends
and feathered bulbs whisper in your depths:
in your pointed crown stars catch the night away,
and altogether (though too much for the mind to hold)
you are a Koh-i-noor lifted to the lips of sight.
Your candid gifts worm the grin up from my heart:
I'm green as you, and there's no winter here.

CYPRESSES AT THE VILLA D'ESTE

'the massive trunks, enduring for ever
the weight of their foliage'   Franz Liszt

Down at the villa Liszt struck and spent
three brooding days under the cypresses;
fed their sobriety, chord and dark chord
into the chromatic plume and toss of funeral.

A piano spills his polished notes: strong fingers
stamp and pull out cypress, which has,
not leaves, but a complex of fern on fern
cut small and smaller, serial of a time
sounding in the waul of the wind in the tops.
Each note and battery of notes
fills out the cypress in our secret lawns,
the gigantic garden grave of midnight frolics.

It's late now, and Liszt's cypress
pushes its foliage into the waiting air
through the mesh of a Japanese radio.
I hear its gigantic nod and sway
passing through, shape and seed,
form into form, pulse rocking a new stem,
pounding out dissonance in the breath
as if we could condense to pure tone
and squeeze up the thread of the tree,

strung and hammered through bole
and smallest interstice of leaf
kilometres above the waving top
in the villa d'Este, in blue Italy.

THE HURDY-GURDY MAKES ITS PITCH

I bring your wooden heart,
its cogs and valves, its many voices.

One forages in the dry leaves,
sacking feet shuffling on sand and stick;

one stirs the rommelpot, the kimmel tub
in the big gut of the hollow man;

one walks a viper, swinging along,
loop left, loop right, tee-tum, tee-tum;

one screams with the love of parrots,
a high romantic with an Arabian zest;

one steals your bones, the femur
and the little toe bones: tosses them

in chorus to the reedy crows. One booms
out where the convicts swing in chains.

And yes, you are right: underneath is the truth,
humming along. I am in your hands,

all together now. We are an earquake,
a soul-ache, a tide in the bedrock.

FLAMENCO

She reels off her own skills
circles the mirror of herself
turns the wrist from its duty
lifts a flame to the sun.

He combs quills into eagles' feathers
knocks out the thumb's opposition
picks the snags out of nerves
flicks the cramped limbs of the soul.

One trapped world spins in another
lost words spell themselves over
the fountain aches for the desert
the formula of light is flung into dark.

THE DEATH'S HEAD GALLIARD

Arc, laser, fire and flare,
hearth, star and ice glow. None catch
this tinder dryback, burnt fireback black
between sockets, this sulk case —
nothing belies me, not light,
not the grave paced state step,
not the gloom of office. I will triple it
chromatic, fast as the spinning worm
mask it. My case at the crown court
is closed, the silk fee settled: now
my scale slides into the minor, on the wire
the rapid harmonics skip out of sight.

Ever yours, fondlings, dear ones,
your workhorse, bonehorse, your fancy.
I glide over gloom lakes cracking the time,
splash ashen waters, clout headlands,
fart like backfire down deep wells.
Night stalks my firework fingers,
blacks your workhouse, bonehouse.
I'm the hobby that grinds your days:
in three and in six, this side and that,
your caper, your shout, your show.

THE VOICE OF THE CARNYX

Reared over the ridge on rough shoulders, tribal terror
comes the carnyx, the boar-headed gem-eyed blaster,
hackles up, brass tongue rattling in the war blaze.

The barbed boar in the sky bellows a courage-queller;
the battle-blare of the bully stampedes the enemy,
skull-dazed, trumpeted into the baleful mouth of hell.

Cooled now by long soaking in the mild bog acid
of Banff, by careful study inch by inch fleshing up
the flaking relic & its Celtic delicate work, woken

and carried hostage into a velvet hall, broadcast
by a college craftsman, a music shifter amused
by its neck bristles, its enormous elemental harmonics

tamed to a new music, released from blurting carnage
to find its inward coils of sound, to toy with the rush
and skirmish of instruments, not knowing how it is

made to answer to a new air, a new death,
its electric & chemical carriers silent,
the Blah of the last day all the nearer for that.

The Carnyx: Reconstructed Celtic battle-horn, Radio 3, 2002.

41

EAST OF HERE

lies the sharp place,
where the cold wind coils its wit,
where the cords of the river run.
East puts out a finger to the cheek,
lucid as ice. New studies beckon:
a pearl cabinet of little drawers.
To the east special things remove, furled
into the unfound space of the shell,
touches of piano rush high in the register,
ting of chandeliers swaying in the wind.

No train reaches, not the two-carriage 6am
which reverses at Ely and stumbles
backwards through Norfolk, though
colour flakes to smoke and shale, collects
in the black of a standing tree. Crows
flap once round a field in wet flannel air
as we slide through Sheppea Hill, Brandon,
Eccles Road, Wymondham, small halts
slapped out of mud. Cattle mope on dykes
in unreachable marsh: telegraph poles keel.
Track, hoardings, shed, chemical silos,
Lignacite, ash tree, smashed. Stringy pines,
silos, foreign barns, suspicious caravans.
It never goes far enough: deposits me flat
at Attleborough and Spooner Row.

Even if I strike out to the Viking shore
the pieces fly apart. East holds its place,
a flinch of light in the corner of the eye,
a morning's spill of clear sight. It nudges,
knocks in the ribs. Always to the left
on the North-South of the spine
brightness harbours, spurned, restless.

SEA-SCAPE

Penned here in wool and grey upholstery
I long for the white house,
the quiet walls and recess,
the candid glass and space
between galleries and shutters.

My white house will flash out
how the sea is cracking Britain open
along its crab rancid fissures,
creeping along brackish lochs
with its fingering tides.

How it will split us,
and oh how we will care for one another
when we take ferries and rowboats
to visit to shop to gaze
from our huge islands of Scotland and Cumbria,
Wolds and Wales and Wash and Anglia,
Weald and Wessex, negotiating the eddies
of islets, Wigtown and Wirral and Man.

Here on the plain
the wash will surge up the motorways,
sluicing out services, sliproads,
scouring the grubby tarmac.
White waves will foam up malls,
licking up the escalators.
And over all the wearied flatlands
the wind will sing and sing.

The flint which shucks a gallery of light
will crash in the storm
and sea salt will cake at our feet in blocks
for the preservation of the British
from bone-ache, upholstery, the rot of wallpaper.

REGISTERING THE ORGANIC SMALLHOLDING

A steep place. Thirty acres divide the wind,
the cloud-race splitting round Maidenpap
to lour across Solway mud. A land rusting
under pines. Winter-salted light roughens shadows,
picks out iron in the rocks, orchid in the swamp.
A land glimpsing, changing under cloud rim
and sudden shower. A nest of streams
flying at night from the winded stars.

Dry dikes mark out the farms,
gate-rayed, gorsed-in, jigsaw-locked.
Currency's the swing of muscle and boot grip,
the tackling idea, deft touch and handy spare.
The lights of ten-mile-neighbours lay a trace
across bogfoot and glen. Ice strips a carcass
in the burn: small deer tremble and slip
into wet woodland, rousing lurchers to riot.

No land wastes: Tamworth Reds root out bracken
cleaner than the plough; they blaze in fields,
hide-banging man-humoured enormous bearers.
A subtle coloured Shetland flock defies dogs
and sense, havocs vets bills. Ten geese march
the fields, routing riff-raff ducks, layabout hens.
Living close to the human house milking goats
speak sweetly, love and quarrel, fuss over food.

Smallholding's a civil world of trial.
Outdoors, mud and scarecrow hours:
indoors, books, music, cookery, computers.
This is working town blood up on its feet,
outfacing centuries, making honey, veg,
milk, eggs, lamb, chicken, wool; tight &
trim as the estuary to the slim stalking bird.

II TRAVELLING THROUGH THE NEWS, 2001

I'm driving south, hunted down the A1
by dirty luck; distant smoke distracts
and the wipers fling snowflack left, right.
It's March 20, and would be Spring.

Speed scarcely holds fear down. Tomorrow
soldiers may *relish a task*, firing out a devil
raised in slaughterpens. Ministers, like Leviticus,
count out compensation for life lost,

but it is only life lost. What stinks in Britain is this —
we don't have time to mess about doing blood tests,
attending to people too small for policy,
matters acute as words turned silky

with the smell of milking goats, cadences
caught from a woman moving gentle about piglets,
this one and that, squealing in my tyres.
A poem's of no account dead in the files

when dead things burn in fields. A virus wants
to breed, eat cheap and fling the packaging away,
so this is no more than the one message
that will not infect, as I stick to big roads

between factories and ports, and fear
for lambs, and weeping men, and suicides.
It will not come to that. *This one's an easy job*.
People grin back at pigs. The snow gets worse.

III   EASTER 2001

Each night the wrenching clock
ticks to the MAFF update. Coffee
tastes of aloes and rain deafens.

The map's abrupt and local,
throws its white circle round,
chills your spine before you can turn.

The kids born this long week
to the milking goats: four Tamworths
and their raucous litters.

The cream-coloured goat steps out
of the dark shed, a shapely light.
Her raw scent lies in the hay.

Finally it is the lamb, fresh as paint,
who bears no weight, a small animal
who takes the soother to its head.

There must be no trouble with Rome,
no loss of exports. In Galloway's black hills
the air is silent and stinks by Friday.

THE BRITTLING OF THE DEER

Made all of triangles upon the grass,
hoof and rump and pointed head perk
by the forest road, a cappuchino swirl
in the broad green cup of Galloway.

There's a gentle man upon the road tonight,
a maker of newsletters, a community man,
driving to town where the Buddhists meet,
keen to disarm the double-bladed heart,
the soft sweatered, the bald and the hairy,
skimming the soul out into the pool of life.

A rough night: the wind slices round Maidenpap,
shaking the moon caught in the deer's eyes,
dark as the still water pooled in bog and peat.
Sudden headlights flay the woodland and she bolts,
bang into the Volvo. Dismay shoots that good man:
he strokes the blank muzzle, weeps for the bright thing,
but folds it, careful, into the car, where it dangles
a cooling hoof from under a crocheted blanket.

He takes it to his neighbours high on the hillside,
circled by barn and byre. One skins the beast, knife
rummaging through tissue layered like lace and muslin.

Slit the slot of the throat, grasp the first stomach,
scrape up the flesh. Legs and skin off;
break into the belly, draw the bowels out, tenderly.
Separate gullet from the wind-pipe, and out with the guts.
Cut out the shoulder joints but keep the sides intact.
Open the breast, neatly into two, start again at the neck,
open the carcass to the fork. The membranes of neck and
                                                    ribs,

all the offal of the back-bone cut free in one piece.
Loosen the folds of the thighs, cut the carcass in two,
then head and neck off. Cut the sides away from the
                                                    backbone
and fling the fair skin to the dogs, with liver, lights and
                                                    tripe.

Sleepless in Galloway the unhappy man of causes,
his pointed hat folded on the newel post:
sleepless the skinner, gripped by the deer-ticks
rehousing their fat blood circles in his anguished pelt,
but where the deer sleeps no-one knows.
Out in the Stewartry a thousand pine-trees moan
and small life leaps and rants by rock and burn.

LISTENING FOR GIANTS

When Joe was a boy he lay flat on the moor,
ear to the dry grass, catching their groans
hunkered down in the boulders.
Lost, late in the mist he heard,
shivering the soles of his boots, snores
ramp the earth in her cold sleep.

Getting home from school he found gasps
tumbling the lilac tree in the yard,
lifting wet sheets. Coming into town
he whistled their tunes pointed in the walls
of factories with fingernail gates, heard them
clacking in sheds, weaving the threads of trees.

He was terrified when the conductor
crooked a yellow elbow over the falling house,
deafened by dentistry with jackhammers,
the steamroller packing the filler in,
hurting the nerves of houses. Big diggers
shunted his dreams, rebuilt his town.

When he left home they filled the junctions
with the pounding of trucks, clogged
every artery with tailback and hooting.
The tyretracks of their Formula One
left a long cemetery. Their sex cries
filled the stadium, rang the air of each precinct.

Learning their speech was worse,
the guttural sounded a slow geology,
dipthongs cumbered his tongue,
vocatives flew rapid as dragonflies.
In middle-age he made a dictionary, noting
the tremor in May, the grind of the moon.

He managed clumsy retorts in the garden,
but cared less in time. His pulse rattled
alongside theirs, and when they left him
with nowhere to go he lay down silent
between them, and Earth ate him lovingly,
attentive, thorough as a dog with a bone.

AND THE NATION SLEEPS DOWNSTAIRS

Heatwave, and the days are jammed
deadcentre, thirty degrees and stasis.
Thoughts and words are doled with sweat,
the sun drumming us out of our heads.
We slug along on fruit and water,
moving the one British fan about,
waiting in turn to shower again.

In the impossible bed
I feel your heat jump the gap
a centimetre from touch;
sex lies on a mottled slab.
The *Sunday Mirror* pronounces —
no-one can sleep and no-one's making it.
So it's not just us (it never is).

At last the calendar clicks,
a gross bumping of aerial systems
and it's over, the engines cranking up,
gridlock slipping off into town,
and we arrive home late,
wash our names and faces,

whoop at sleeping through the night,
and these are *sleeves* and this is *soup*
and it's our thirtieth anniversary
and we're on our fifth bed
exchanging glues again, impacted like wrestlers.

Whatever sweltered leaves no sign.
Not earth damp between grasses —
not the frogs nudged out by rain —
not the morning air of washed cotton —

and not your skin which coasts on mine
in our deep channels, our trade routes
with their reliable lights blinking
day after day in easy rhythm,
saving us from splintering wreck
on our way north, where the ice is.

POST-MENOPAUSE

Finally dumped the clown
capering away in the corner;

kicked the kiddy conjurer out
with his damn balloons;

snapped the red filter off the lens.
Here's to holding hands in the park again.

POEM IN A DRAWER

I ended up fleshing it out, as you do,
with something I'd found in a drawer
                    Don Paterson *The Reading*

Probably a wooden kitchen table,
beech or pine, waxy, wide-grained;
one drawer each side
offering a round wooden knob:
it sticks and grates as it opens,
hangs askew: you forget it's there.
But a kid might find it, lunchtime.

Inside, a pair of stiff garden gloves,
a rattle of dried unidentifiable flora,
two obsolete kitchen gadgets,
a raffia mat, a dead dog's lead,
a pot of copper coins,
one tin of dry polish,
a bunch of keys to lost doors.
All quiet and easy, settled with itself
like Miss Marple, bright cottage lady.

But poems don't live in drawers,
and kitchens come in flat slabs, fitted:
fifteen drawers: this sort of knife,
that sort of knife, the plastic bags,
the garlic press. Poems sort in files,
notebooks, store upright and electric.

Yet suppose a soul could hang on,
chiming in a kitchen drawer
while categories blaze, files and boxes
burn up in pride and presumption;

and suppose, when the cupboards crash down
and all the murderers are hanged
you find a pulpy bag, obscurely strung —
it might conceal a poem,
its folds a little furred, its soft appeal
all meant for you, and never sent.

THOSE PICTISH, CELTIC THINGS

Those chambers, basalt rocks,
those beehives, stones and brochs —
a postcard from The Skelligs, and
one more friend moved by silence
to mewing words.
I'm standing in Burrian,
Evie, Birsay, Burness,
standing in Orphir like a stone.

Marram grass and black bog rush
whistle on the shore
in Papil, Mail and Lerwick,
where the seal patterns itself,
where king and birdman beckon
and say *Forget. Here is no time.*

Dashed from home by white waves
we visit settlements of times
we have no name for, lay hands
on earth's bouldered overflowing heart,
make lenten dreams
of oats and fish on the dry slab.

The still air damps the running pulse,
opens our clenched sight.
The skua's cry is spare and modern,
the cave's low discords
pulling at the gut. Touching graveslab,
hearthstone, porch and cross
we feel the push of peace
like the breeze bringing the sea home,

not fetched from the back-lit faery hall
of makebelieve and loss
but in our packing up we brought it,
buried deeper than Columbanus
in gravelled surges, in our footsole
hidden like the speck of quartz
which checks our feet, makes us limp
and catch our breath on salt Iona.

But this is the rock that will not open
for any photograph, stones with no register
of ferry times, no care for our leaving.
Being so, in spite of all respect
maybe we're here to carve our names
across the silica stars on these blind sills.

Yet see
        how what's written in the lichen
weathers us,
            salmon leaping in air,
                            runes
cut cleaner than we can dream
of the world we hide our password in,
in cities, in dull towns with Latin names,
the stone we bring to open with our lunchbox
here in the roofless house again, attending,
needing the rude unlocking of the sea.

VARIATIONS ON WALSINGHAM

How should I your true love know
  From another one?
By his cockle hat and staff
  And his sandal shoon.

He is dead and gone, lady,
  He is dead and gone,
At his head a grass-green turf,
  At his heels a stone.

Anon, to the tune 'Walsingham', Hamlet 4.5

I

Alas, look here, a girl in white all lily-sweet,
boldly singing the ill-dressed songs
of fathers and lovers and what-may-be.

The shallows spread her marriage-bed;
her song laps the reeds. The slow current
licks her into silence like a mother's tongue.

Downstream of the curious court Sir Walter
catches the tune from the willow, weaves
a nowhere song to this Bess and that,

another candle in another bloody wind.
Love likes not the falling fruit, From the withered tree.
The sea casts him up from his golden dream,

sandals awash with little shells, earns him quietus,
a pillow block. Gertrude lies forever in a faint:
Elizabeth and Mary dwell in the brick of homage.

II

And when our bottles and all we
Are fild with immortalitie

Raleigh

Incense and plaster stiffen their sailing shroud.
Inside the shrine a plastic box illuminates
the stained Turin face, a not-what-it-seems

by a master in the art of unacceptable truths,
of a man forgotten as he came from the holy land,
anywhere where news is reliable, but not to be borne.

The Milky Way's fogged over now, no kind of guide:
tourists watch pilgrims for sudden genuflections.
Handy dandy, which is the fool and which the king?

It beggars belief, this capital shrine to the one
who bore the one who died. Sons are lost,
Elsinore and elsewhere: *you must sing down a-down.*

Mary's ghost croons in the candle light,
a *Lachrimae Verae* under her waxen breath;
no dancing on Norfolk's reed and flinted flats.

III

I have plaied so long with my fingers
I have beaten out of plaie all my good fortune
John Dowland

Ophelia drops the lute she little plays,
lingers, the boards creaking with pity,
afloat on the fervent waters of applause.

The real dances with the true, Bankside, Fetter Lane,
Whitehall and Denmark: heroes travel cold seas
and colder measures. The Globe sets its ghost train out

in good King Christian's land, where folly court
staggers round the best of London's music-men,
expensive exile, king of the heartsease.

(Musicians in our livery die bloodily enough,
but that was in Father's time and though
this one's a Catholic we shall simply ignore him)

Song and strutting step, people and court,
pulses fired into the disconsolate mind
to flaunt at fingers' end in firework fancy.

IV

All pilgrims are glad to get home, tired of
the one-way traffic of an Anglian village,
tired of foppery goldmines and miracles

but from the radio the notes swirl
in a feathering tide from the mannered lute
so how shall, how shall we forget, on the road

to Walsingham the bravery when Dowland
delivers the loop of wit around and under
like the green man's tongue of leaves,

the speaking tune & seven variations
for all to follow, rueful, sweet as rosemary,
each more rapid, chromatic, dislocated

and swept to the home key of the vibrating shell,
for all artists are courtiers to the Antic but then
we can build   monuments   out of thin air.